Devil at the Crossroads

2

Devil at the Crossroads

Poems by Paula Coomer

For Dr. Ed Whiting
- Be careful of the devil
at the crossroads.
Paula Coomer

Lewis-Clark Press
Lewiston, Idaho

ACKNOWLEDGMENTS:

Certain of these poems have appeared previously, often in earlier versions. Thanks to the editors for allowing their use here:

Versions of "First Aid," "Dove Creek," "American Beauty," "The Fugitive," and "Patrons" appeared in the chapbook *Dove Creek*, Spore Productions, Vashon Island, WA, 1994;

"Glenda the Good Witch," *Aura Literary Arts Review*, Birmingham, May 1999;

"Sack Lunch," *The Advocate*, Plainsville, New York, October 1999;

"Chance Divination," *Voices on the Wind*, Bisbee, Arizona, June 2003;

"A Philosopher of Cousins," "At a Bar in Spokane," "Ethnic Cleansing," "Maturity," and "Rebirth, Repast," *Meghbarta* (www.meghbarta.org), November, 2003.

Cover art and concept is by Gabe Hathaway, adapted from a 1912 photograph, "Old South Road Near Mittagong," by Harold Cazneaux.

Lewis-Clark Press is a Northwest subsidiary of Sandhills Press, independent publisher of Great Plains poetry since 1979. Address all correspondence to:
Lewis-Clark Press
Kimberly Verhines, Series Editor
Mark Sanders, Associate Editor
Humanities Division
Lewis-Clark State College
Lewiston, ID 83501

Printed in the United States by Morris Publishing
3212 East Highway 30
Kearney, NE 68847
1-800-650-7888

CONTENTS:

For the Archangel, all my Davids,
and Richard

DEVIL AT THE CROSSROADS

1.
heartlessness is an art.
bonds in pieces that do not embrace anymore.
ragged as a broken candle.
taint that smells of silver spoon.

2.
I once found a cradle rocking under a sliced moon.
it looked like a thing of my longing.
when I wasn't watching the dandelion beneath it went to seed.
everything blew away.
it only took one of my breaths.

3.
my mother warned me not to shave.
coddling need makes it more insistent, she said.
how could I survive without that advice.
there are few casual warnings on which one can depend.

4.
there is a place for lonesomeness.
a nest through which you weave a twig.
soften it with feathers until it is time to fly.

5.
I have never seen the devil at the crossroads.
but he has blue eyes.
sometimes I dream regret is a stop sign.
what if it is a sin to remain uncomfortable.

FIRST AID

Scrapbooks should be recalled, and some anxious
junior clerk hired to re-label them scabbooks.
That's what we store between the covers. Lacerations.
Abrasions. Avulsions. And their keloid scars.

POTLATCH

If you give the government fingerprints, prepare to be whisked
away—maybe to the Indians—bleeding shiny in your mother's
denial basket. Say grace for silver mirrors, asking—girl, girl, who
is this animal, this figure of ochre and black? Carrying fire to no
one, clothed with skins from no hunt, smudged with juice from
ceremonies without grapes?

All that dancing. All those eyes. Withered limbs fling spark
smaller than dust, sand smaller than grit, teeth smaller than a voice.
Words strict with music, but no bells like my name.

Cut to now. In a bed not made of roses. Seems the only rock I
smell is concrete. Seems I smell fired meat rotted in the middle of
dead fish.

Struggling eyes: find me back with them. My ancient ones.

THE WAY OF BARE FEET

All along I've said: when dawn arrives
higher than my head, it will be time to stand, time
to wake, time to put my feet on the hard rock.

Somehow they've grown un-callused. Ivory, satiny,
unlined flesh of a wobbly child. *Shoes*
will eventually make her stand, advising aunts might say.

Hard soled, high topped, soft flat cords laced
through eyelets.

Tying shoes to unhard feet will keep them
that way. But the baby will be steadied.

FADED RED AND ASPHALT GRAY

Colors come without desire fronting them. Like the brand new
old-time version of an antique cheese box, painted by the wife
of the fire department chief; the quilt crafted by a woman member

of an Idaho tribe; a wool rug, handspun, dyed with vegetable
juice from a weaver friend of an artist friend who introduced
me to Bartlett's quotations. So much for yellow fruit.

More of the same from elsewhere: sixty dollars
worth of reprints of the Nez Perce at Celilo, before the dams
took away the falls and the salmon; a carved tourist angel

from Guatemala and a mask from there with empty
sinus holes waiting for feathers; a mandala from nineteen-eighty
made from a bicycle hoop while waiting out a pregnancy

and I have added more than two illegal hawk feathers since;
my only set of bedsheets, washed every calendar page
whether they need it or not. These are the things of my rodeo.

From the center of this I play hooky with my red heart,
read and die in solitude, long for a bit of difference.
These are my life made material, my farthest soul made manifest.

They are and are not the colors of contentment.

ETHNIC CLEANSING

Take a half barrel of whiskey, I mean
half a whiskey barrel, and lay dirt
first, then ponies of posies. Not ponies
like the horses they grow into, but black

square cartons, little four-hole egg cartons
filled with their own tiny dirt and hobbled
roots—black—because they're made from
some distant aspect of crude oil, hillbilly

crude like Jethro's and Ellie Mae's
and my own daddy's.

Then you'll have a nice spot of color,
a place for weeds to grow around
making it hell to mow, but the yard'll
look just like the Jones's, with trees

cut down bare except for spots
left to grow shade and juleps, because
they—like we—ache for savannah,
a place familiar to our apian ancestors.

THE SOUL OR THE COG

Lay me belly over granite, feet first, dangling
in mountain water. Crisp. Chilly. Defy this
western experience by thinking silly, city girl
thoughts, draining blood from head to toe.

At the heart of the matter is a song slung blue
and high, defying altitude, hitting ping! ping!
between us and stars, the glossy outside of this
marble no one sees except from way far out.

What is the thought? Did the machine come
from the spider web, the spider from the gun?
Or was it all so far past no one remembers
which hatched first, the soul or the cog?

BLAMELESS

To be a tree:
to stand with branches out sucking
juice from the ground until it is cold
enough for leaves to fall and be naked,
then have them scraped up, raked up,
and burned while smoke rises
high enough to smell.

To be a camel:
to wander the humped desert
ignorantly making snot and spit
in the place of no water.

To be a mushroom:
to live where earth is damp
and bloom best beneath
dead logs after dark.

DOVE CREEK

Hear the drum. See the echo.
Past our bones. Past our birth.
Past the dirt.

Back to the moon.

Hear the moon. See the drum.

Drum.
Drum.
Drum.

Of us all.

* *

In the eyes of wolf beats
the heart of dove. And tears
flood the creek stones.

ATOP

If night were a guardrail,
the road falling down the mountain,
      like dna spirals, spiraling
      relentlessly down
      like it does,
then it could also be a hallway,
      or a stairwell, stairstep, spiral staircase
      falling to anyplace,
falling like an apple peel
(slip, slip
drop)
from the core.

FLOWERGIRL

She was four, Cinderella pink in tulle to the floor and leotards, Prince
Charming in the mirror, calling to dance, the kissing light from
flashbulbs, the promise of patent leather down linen aisles between the
pews of Mt. Zion Methodist where the neighbor's daughter and their
neighbor's son pledged 'til death do us part, the most exciting event
altogether in her calendar life.

They would read about it in the Lanesville Gazette: Davey Riley in his
big boy suit not dropping the ring. The organ player with satin gloves
and blue stiff hat playing what the singer sang. Each one in place, just
like rehearsal, just like dreaming, just like the movies.

Except for Cinderella.

Forgot, she said. Forgot to take rose petals from the dimestore basket
and toss them. Forgot, listening to her patent leather footsteps, to pave
the way safe for them, a sacrifice of fragrance, the guild of roses, from
the candlelit world of mommies and daddies, into the night, the night
that looked like day and sun, darkless only for the moment, its reality
sprung from a tomorrow with a throat, a swallow to make them forget
their promises, turn them into people too lazy to stay whole.

No going back and redoing it, her daddy said. You only get one chance
to do it right. Standing in front of him, perfect in a pink dress, in front
of the man who made her, sure it just couldn't be, the princess girl
pivoted dancer toes into the sanctuary, into a place named holy,
to dream seated alone on a church pew, of the world righted, the world
as it should be, the world if she hadn't forgotten to throw the flowers, if
she hadn't made a flowergirl mistake so big.

CHANCE DIVINATION

One morning when I was five and sitting high
on the Sears and Roebuck catalogue, my mother
put coffee instead of hot chocolate
in front of me on the metal table.

Oh. She said. I thought you were your father.

Later that day we were canning peaches.
I came running back to the house
with the speckled turkey roasting pan
still full of pits and peelings because a snake
was under the redbud tree. She switched me
with a switch I watched her cut and peel, after
she couldn't see the snake herself. She said,
lying's same as stealing in the eyes of god
and his son jesus.

RELICS

From my bed on the living room couch
I heard him. A rat worked the night shift
in the laundry room, and Mom had to carry
hot water in there in a chipped porcelain bowl
from the stove in the kitchen every time
my underwear got dirty from my being afraid
of choosing to go to the outhouse in the dark
over the chipped white pot with a lid
where the rat waited.

I saw a letter and a picture in the newspaper
about antiques. A woman asking if her porcelain
treasure was a soup tureen. No, the columnist
answered. Merely a chamber pot.

GLENDA THE GOOD WITCH

It's easy to be famous in Edwardsville, Indiana,
if you can spell principal and principle and know
which one is your *pal*. This you get to tell
to the sixth graders and the fifth graders
and the fourth graders, while pretending moth wings
aren't flapping in the hot chocolate you drank
for breakfast, and bumping against the Cheerios,
same as they did on the first day of first grade
and the first day of second grade
and the first day of third grade, all this
in the dress your mother made from a flour sack.

HELL ON VISITORS

A.M. early on Sunday watching snowflakes,
you'll be glad for steam-burned hands ladling
grape juice last summer fresh from the sieve,
where green pulpy seeds and skins pouted betrayal
betrayal and loss,
decadent in their emptiness.

Nosey, shouldn't-she-be-cloistered aunt,
hobbling in from nowhere, nickering lip-stained
cigarette between her horse's teeth. (Only one!
And that after dinner every day for the past
forty years of my life!)
And her dress always dead blue rayon
and her shoes (call 'em high-toppers—
I do!) on feet to make a buffalo feel cheated.

Where was she when the canner tipped, spilling
(mercy jesus) blue juice all over our new stove?

FIRSTBORN

It was not uncommon for him to show me
his fishing lures, in the wee hours of morning
upstairs before he went to milk
when everyone below was asleep,
and to talk about them slick and rubbery,
looking just like worms, or bugs with hooks.

One day, when I fried my back on the electric fence,
which kept the livestock separate from the house
and barn, he comforted me in the smokehouse,
which meant he was better than some,
who could only afford to cure with salt,
but not as well off as others,
who took their meat to town.
Opening my mouth was easy.
Tasting it was hard.
Thinking about it the next morning over Easter ham
was even worse.

BEFORE SUMMER

Lizards lived under the step in the summer.
And the devil's walking stick climbed the sycamore
next to the locusts which had their own trees
and sometimes escaped at night, leaving only their shells,
which we harvested to heap on the monument of snail shells
we collected from the pile of gravel
next to the evil forest
past which we walked on the devil's gravel road
a quarter mile to catch the school bus, knowing
the wicked witch of the west might fly over any minute,
or a tornado.

The school bus driver was my friend, until the day
Prince ran too close to his bumper, even though
he wasn't supposed to follow me, even though
it was huge and yellow and he should have seen it,
and cut his nose.

When a hunter came by and said he was looking
for a good dog, I gave Prince away, not knowing
I would miss him.

WINDS ALOFT

I would know what to call winds from an aircraft
if winds from an aircraft were a natural thing. Even if
they didn't hold me aloft in this riveted beast, sandwiched
between inseparable wings and a silvered belly, shedding
the sun's glitter shadow on the water beneath.

Winds from childish stories blew hard and steady
enough to clear a little pig's house, making wolf
and his story beastly, keeping me afraid of invisible
things strong enough to hold me up while blowing
me away.

A mother can be like that—at least she has the teeth—
teeth to separate a heart into tattered pieces, tattered like
rags in the wind drying fastened to a clothesline, held aloft
in my innocent days by wire knotted to nails pounded into oak
limbs from which winds aloft brought tattered leaves
and winged seeds—dependable, natural aircrafts—
for a common Indiana girl to chase whirling and winded
to the ground.

EXCEPT I HAVE NO RUSSIAN

I was born with this regard for birth. This ache
for corpus cavernosum, a translation of the biological,
the *ping ping* of my own flapping exhaust machine
spitting out ball bearings from my nested collection
of potential people since before my allotment began.

Nothing more than a painted matrjoshka, lathed
by machine, a tourist trap, a trinket, a doll inside a doll
inside a doll inside a doll, assessing possibility (heat-seeking
genetics) for a cog, a gear, a silent energy converter.

Sometimes I think I am made of people. Only
the littlest one, the middle of the middle, as far inside
as a good girl can peek, into where my grandmother's
grandmother's grandmother's grandmother opened up
and fell away, the same as her daughter and her daughter
and her daughter and her daughter and her daughter
and her daughter and her daughter.

My own daughter I pulled out head first and popped it
off like a weed, a seed dropped un-kerneled to the ground.

It takes guts to prevent a miracle, so I did.

So much for mater familia. But it is so American:
killing the plot of our own; killing the artists; killing
them before they fill the plots in Stone Cemetery.

ROCKHOUNDS

(for Daddy)

I want you to come here with a little pick
whose head is held by a hard, wooden handle
somewhat smaller than your head,
somewhat smaller than my hand.

I want you to come here with a little pick
to break rocks, rocks pushed from under deep
Idaho, Idaho that was once Mazama, rocks that
broken open seem to bleed, make you bleed,
if you are not careful of them.

I want you to come here with your little pick,
your bag of rocks, to sit with me by this creek
bed, to see how not only still waters run deep,
how deep an ankle is, how deep a knee, how easy
it is to walk until all this water is over my head.

I want you to sit with me
by this creek bed, you with your little pick, me
with mine, sharing our bag of rocks, speaking
quietly, to find the meaning of garnet bleeding,
garnet born of pick and shovel, hand-raked
from almost clay, almost sand, garnets almost
the same as marble, marble feet, garnet feet,
statues made of stone.

PLAID FLANNEL

This is the disparity of survival:

1) it is hard holding on in wind,
   throughout seasons and blood red moons,
   but letting go is the same as death.

2) when it is cold enough,
   everything green yellows and falls off.

3) winter is the champion of family men
   who have gained a reason
   to rise from the table and chop brown wood.

4) wool keeps the body warmest,
   although it is weighty enough when wet
   to pull one down and under silver water
   no matter the temperature of the air.

5) blood is blue if the color of veins
   straining against the inside of skin can be believed—
   but it is the natural tendency of bleeding
   to be red.

PATRONS

I am 37 in a tavern in Seattle

and the waiter says to me are you
an author

and I say
no I am a writer
(there is a difference)

and he says
what do you write

and I say
I am a poet

that is good
he says
this world really needs
more poets

and I smile
and he smiles
and we connect

and I say
thank you
that is good
to hear

FUNEREAL BEST

I have a hard time
being perfectly dependable.

Once when I was at the far back
of a motorcade launched for my best friend's
death funeral, I turned my headlights off
and veered another way. Not wanting to waste
a good new black dress, I stopped at a western
store and bought cowboy boots to go with it.

The same thing happens every time
a man puts a ring on my finger, it feels
like a crick in my neck—
life becomes a barge without a refrigerator,
no place to go for a cold one,
no place to rest my feet against,
marveling at the mess I ate.

I thought about looking for employment
as an alligator wrestler. They won't notice
if I don't show up for work.

FARGO, FOUR A.M.

It's the Greyhound terminal,
Fargo, four a.m., and you're there
because old female grad students
don't have money for planes
and whatever is outside in the cold
is far more seeable than vending machines
and the women inside with dirty babies.
A bus station prophet leans on the brick
wall across from yours and says,
"You know the next thing
we have to worry about?"
And the yellow earphones
make him look a little crazier,
that and the fact he's beaming proud
of his newly stolen backpack,
just being sociable,
last night's bathroom booze
polishing his lips, headed north
from Denver to Chicago, looking
for his soul, fearful as he is
of the millennium and scientists
breeding computer chips
with DNA.

HAILING LOVE IN MIDDLE-AGE

I imagine what it smells like
to feel a man. At this age,
when cotton feels like alabaster,
charcoal smells like chalk felt
scratching pink and sky blue velvet
on the sidewalk, and after dinner mints
is a phrase for those of us adept
at keeping time by how many there are
left of us sleeping at the table.

Mother, let him dance for me.

HARV JUST AFTER WINTER

(COUNTRY MAN WILL TRAVEL:
Stable, good-natured DWM, 5'8", 150 lbs., 41
looks younger. Singer, songwriter, loves music,
dancing, cooking, sports and raising my 3 kids.
Seeking attractive S/DWF 30-45 with similar
interests. Call me, can't hurt. 8557)

Sunday morning at your place
the first time, after not sleeping with you,
but staying over anyway
because we stretched the night
toward sunbreak by talking until three
after you taught me country swing,
and I was too tired to drive down the mountain,
I wanted to tell you this was the first time
a guy didn't treat me like some other life,
and that forever would go quickly
if it included a little dancing,
and paired hands of fingers
toiling in the Idaho dirt.

I wanted to tell you I saw your name
months ago in a dream, that I thought
you might be a lucky rabbit's foot,
the real Quetzalcoatl,
and that seeing you in the personals column
was in truth an accident
while looking for performance dates
for Arsenic and Old Lace,
and that I only managed
not calling to leave my number
for three days.

But fast talk sometimes scares a guy,
and morning words are clearest
after afterthought.
Better to content me with writing poems,
content me with slow, later promises,
slow sometimes, solitude,
'til that maybe day at the door to your place,
you greeting me gratefully, seeing who I am.

JUST DO IT

Pork bellies. Layers of pork
on my belly; cut it off
and make pork rinds.
Lie, lay, lie on the hot
summer eating watermelons
and let the rinds float
from their pink seeded heavens
away from the grass
with a push of your brown arm
and lay, lie, lay your sweaty chest
on top of my pork belly
to put your seed in me.
Yes, indeed.

                **

If I were on a summer's day
sitting on a beach
and you a dreamsicle on a stick,
not a drop
would reach
the sand.

THE MIRACLE OF HARVEY

The miracle of Harvey was his hands.

Once he pulled a pine bucket full of water
out of a well, pine bucket he made the summer before
from a felled tree, felled by his own ax, ax he made
the summer before from a felled tree, felled because
he pushed it over hard after a big Idaho rain.

The bucket went deep in the well, hung from a rope
he made of bark and yarns twisted from the ewe
he kept in the front lawn to clip down the clover, ewe
he kept to tromp down the weeds, keep down
the mosquitoes and the gnats.

Never tasted water so silver and liquid, as that
from the pine bucket he made out of a felled
tree, felled by his own ax, pine bucket hanging
from a rope he made of bark and yarns
twisted from the ewe he kept in the front lawn
to clip down the clover, lowered down
into the well he dug, well he dug with his own hands,
own hands splitting the earth a fistful at a time, fistfuls
of dirt that before led to nowhere, now heaped
and covered quietly in clover, their undone space
filled with still waters, still waters running deep,
and the coolness he brought me by the bucketful,
in the heat of a long dusty day.

SACK LUNCH

Sitting by a rockfaced cliff, red,
windworn, crevassed, I am privy to a hairline
crack
where a community of ants
is busy lining up bread crumbs
from the lunch I didn't eat—
a sandwich,
layered with mayonnaise and butter
because the meat wagon didn't arrive,
nor the butler
with a tray of cheese,
cold cutlets,
or liverwurst.
I hope they don't make
the same mistake I did,
eating before chewing and swallowing,
without accounting for taste.

DEATH

Boots without feet

Shades without eyes

Lips without teeth

Reed without breath

Heart without wing

I sob

You drum

MENTAL NOTE

When the days are all alabaster and you see
right through them and they leave minus a wisp
and your basket carries only the crumpled petals

of disintegrating blossoms and you wonder
about the relevance of high teas as opposed
to siestas, and no longer believe marketing,

there is not enough spark to interest me.
My body, still beating, warrants putting a foot
in front of it, feeding it, letting it sleep, taking care

when it is sick, and is devastated at the thought
of destroying it, of treating it incautiously, as though
a ginger leaf instead of a carton gold and dear.

FOUR MEN BUILDING A HOUSE

I didn't see it burn, but it did. For days
I watched it stinking where it used to stand
as I walked past afterward—wet, charred
wood smelling like burnt house. It should
have had a smoke alarm. It didn't take much
to get a fire going or last long, a stick house
with plastic toys in primary colors messing up
the yard, a carport full of woodstove wood.

A week or two later some men came to separate
the salvageable from the indistinguishable, douse
the leftovers with kerosene, and strike a match to it. Then
later, after the leaves fell and the snow,
they graded the mud and started over again,
a hole dug in the ground like a hole.

Maybe they found a taproot, something
from which to grow a whole subdivision.
Maybe they found the reason, after the rain
finished, to lift the plastic sheeting
and start nailing things together.

A FLY ALREADY

There's a fly already—
black, winged, fat—
a pharaoh circulating the latex perimeter
of my old glass kitchen window.

Bold, I think, for April.
For a spring that's only been here—
let's see now—a day and a half.

Can only mean his cronies lurk.

Can only mean his harlot wives breed
in bread on a sooty heap
back behind the Comet and Liquid Plumber
under the sink basin
where I haven't scrubbed for most the year
and won't, now,
thinking about maggot babies,
squirmy and wiggly, hatching and hatchling.

It's enough to
let my vocal cords
scream this scream.

SPOKEN LIKE A PHONY POET

I hear like it's raining and it's in the forest.
I hear like no lightning has struck,

like nothing is exploding.
Yet the distance broadcasts a storm.

Must be a measure of consequence
that only wet leaves are awake and softly comforting—

muffling, dampening, tampering with impressions—
softening footprints on a deepening bed.

SPRING VALLEY RESERVOIR

A reservoir is man-made sweetness, a lozenge of metaphor for
heart-parched tongues, tennis shoe welts from dirt paths, fishing line
and old bobbers, lures plucked in haste by fish mouths, and an old
gray muskrat, conscious of the whispers he makes swimming past—
mustn't scare the minnows he's after.

I'm here for the heron, a great grey thing I've seen fly over when
I've felt bad before, coming here as I do to gain perspective on some
injustice or other—me the perpetual victim of soggy will, like
minnows swimming vulnerable, unconscious.

He flies overhead, great pterodactyl wings batting, and he bids me
be like him, in spite of myself. From his height I see clearly—me
sitting pitifully, butt plopped and dusty on a blank bank, forgetting
how much like a minnow I am—a jillion of me, blue and
insignificant coming to the surface reflecting back the sun.

Suddenly, and without alert, heron shoots toward me, dives fast to
grasp one, flying with it wiggling, dripping in his beak—glinting
from being stolen alive.

I focus in on myself, breathing on the beach, make tennis shoes dig
heel ends into hill sand, climbing backward to fern cover. Glancing
over my shoulder to heron swooping low over reservoir for sparkly
seconds, his *sscrreech* and *shwwoosh* mocking me.

Back on gravel I sigh for civilization. I think I've lost need of him.
Heron, silent but with his eye on me, squats brief on seasonless
cattails, shits minnow and consequence flat on a log.

SO MUCH WATER, SO MUCH RAIN

Every day in winter I set the hours on my clock
back by two, take the nap otherwise spent worrying

I was wasting time, waking from branches stark
and lacy black against haze, to summer again and brightness

surprising as the way cut grass smells like red watermelon.
This keeps me far in advance of the charge of living water,

tidal waves that rake and beat along a path of least resistance,
questioning: should I know when it stops and suns

that poppies will thrive in the same ground as forget-me-
nots, one thrusting blue in dirt unneeded by the red

of the other? My only certainty is the swan's step
I take along this passage, muddied from so much water,

so much rain, the lawn shed and waiting to be resod,
breathless as a winter-shiny day.

WHY A POET GOES HOME EARLY

The poet lives for an eclipsed moon,
fallen into obscurity behind earth and sun,
a chorus of dead stone rising red
as wolf teeth dripping blood, my wrist torn
and soaking already muddied ground.

The moon's silver cuffs like love spent,
its circle parted, incomplete and open,
a sequin, shadowing, shiny with expression,
glossy as a zealot's eyes dying in a lost battle
between silver bullet, werewolf, and sun.

GRAVEN IMAGES

Heading down Sixth Street
to Tim's Café for coffee,
I saw two bright orange oranges
in a gutter gray as a snipe—
one round, one conehead,
dimpled butt-up, together
like an eight ball and cue
in the skid-proofing gravel
pushed aside
by the last purposeful snowplow
to come through for Sixth Street.

That's weird enough, I thought,
to write a poem about.

IN SUPPORT OF PERSERVERANCE

When the hammock grows thready and the yellow wallpaper falls off and it's gut music versus NPR and tapping feet, the whole damned world percolating again, try bending over a bluebell or blue bonnet. Try not fading into blue, rather zone in on the less obvious—that blue is perched on stems and leaves green as can be in a sea of grass, and underneath the earth is brown, and the sky overhead may be blue or may not, but all of it together with the dread pumping of a human heart equals perfect dew and the grass at the green heart of it all makes blue stand out clear as crystal. Even an ocean of bluebells would remain hidden, were it not for the ebb and surf of green stems underneath.

JACK

His last dime spent on coffee for a blonde

She wonders where he'll get

Seventeen bucks

When they raise his rent

À LA MODE

When couples walk, she mostly does
the speaking,
cartoon-faced, evidencing the tiara,
the pearl of his attention. She marks territory,
pees on trees and hydrants, in case another
of her species and gender is within pheromone
distance.

Mostly, it's limp noodles, a shaking of the lint
bag,
consumed as she is by his vacuum.

AT A BAR IN SPOKANE

I snorted cocaine with a man
who said, "It only makes your nose bleed
if you cut it with a razor blade." Smiling
at his own joke, he told me how his mother
locked him in a closet and fed him Oreos
and thorazine and told the principal
he was sick when he was only fat.

**

There are bottles like soldiers stacked
against a peaceful ceiling. Each holds
a drug of choice: pick your poison,
a stairway to heaven. None holds
the ticket out of here and on a night
below zero there's not enough
to draw a crowd.

BENCHMARK

Someone told me to dance like no one is looking, and that it's
Wyeth hawking Van Gogh every time somebody picks up a brush.
Bends it to sacrilege, then, comparing one to another, since both
appear content hanging side by side in a gallery.

The same can be said of feeding pigeons.

Old men with socks pass pleasant days seated on municipal benches
feeding the flock from brown paper sacks of seed, yet some consider
both pests. Police people in blue suits with night sticks in daylight
shoo away men and birds, an act not considered ungraceful or
unnecessary to those with briefcases, but I struggle with it.

It's like having a baby in a manger who was more intriguing to
corporate sponsors than to the peasantry, until, of course, someone
starred him in a commercial. That was the day looking up turned
more appealing than looking to the ground.

So one fine day when the officers have nothing left to do, they'll
look for the park bench, and our children will let them sit because
cable TV will have taught them the importance of seeds and birds,
in spite of our failure to pass it on. That is the way of needful
things, the way sediment was meant to be.

A PHILOSOPHY OF COUSINS

Life is a limiter
whereby we borrow transgressions
from one another and lay down
passages, presumably to take us
from one place to another, like a road,
a train track, a cushion of air.

Alongside might be a mushroom field
where they grow life from recycled cow
dung. What a path to take that would be.
But how sensible.

In dominant society are many masks. Boring,
but pretty, and plentiful. You can wear and discard,
wear and discard, as many as you like, but
it will not save your soul.

In the deserts, I have heard, are people who no longer
have sex. Not enough of earth to stick around for,
they say. Not so blatant as suicide, but just as effective,
although harder on the feet, walking around on all that
hot, sun-baked sand every day.

Useless pain.

I keep telling myself: there is always poetry.
But it seems a shame to waste such woeful words
on forgotten ears. Am I afraid of Virginia Woolf? I am
afraid of being Virginia Woolf. And afraid of not.
She was my mother's keeper. It was she
who begat me.

BEFORE MY CROWN

If had been born into other than the known
world, would I or the world be different?

If I were adorned less than this,
would I be less adorned?

If I looked other than any of my selves,
would I be inclined to screech about it?

None of us is different.

IN THE KITCHEN

Intentions are fog and my heart a sink. These feet
fear their own stockings. My clothes are silent
smoke and so I lay me down, a kitten in old age
whose coat is tangled with birth. Surround this heart
and hold it to the flame, until my brassiness
knows why I chose only to make marmalade.

FIRST TENTATIVE MOMENTS

After rattling around a matchbox
for some odd years, beginning
with falsehoods and ending with creation,
a slow journey without destination
would be cheaper.

Hope often marries ideals
but inevitably divorces itself.

Courting chance
is a limitless freightline.

MATURITY

We are ripe when we yield
to gentle pressure, when we are
no longer afraid and fear
has lost its grip.

We are stable
when our feet are staked
shoulder width apart
and we are no longer staked
in what is at stake
for us.

We are able
when we confess our abilities
and passion is no longer
the only thing that makes us
passionate.

And we are healthy
when health is no longer
threatened
by that which we put into us,
but is demonstrated by that which
comes out of us.

BROOD

Life is a series of x-marked spots.
Childhood ink connects the dots.
Fairy tale crumbs mark the trails we trace,
looking for mama and her porridge

**

We were raised by hollow people
who kept us hollow by bleeding us,
and so we seek a place of comfort
where hollow people keep us hollow
by bleeding us, and yet find comfort
in childish things and create rituals
of denial to avoid admitting to them,
while insisting we cannot go home.

**

Let these things be made manifest,
that all men might remove their earrings
and come to the aid of their country-time
drink mix. Mama, did you say they call
that Tang?

ABOUT THE AUTHOR:

Paula Coomer is a short story writer, novelist, and poet currently living in Lewiston, Idaho. An active advocate of the writing arts, she has participated in numerous conferences in the Northwest, as writer-in-residence and as a symposium leader. She holds an MFA in Creative Writing from the University of Idaho and taught for a number of years at Washington State University, where she conducted the Visiting Writers Series. She is now writing full-time. *Devil at the Crossroads* is her first full-length collection of verse.